THE KEY TO
DUBAI

UNLOCKING THE STORY OF A CITY AND ITS CULTURE

Written and illustrated by
Liliane van der Hoeven

To my parents Jan and Angèle Wouters
– grateful for everything

For Eric and our children Mare, Feline and Robin
– to cherish our family life in Dubai

The Key to Dubai
1st Edition 2015

Published by Explorer Publishing & Distribution
PO Box 34275, Dubai
United Arab Emirates
+971 (0)4 340 8805
retail@ask**explorer**.com
ask**explorer**.com

To buy additional copies of this or any other of Explorer's award-winning titles, visit askexplorer.com/shop.
Special discounts are available for bulk purchases at askexplorer.com/corporate.

ISBN 978-1-78596-003-1

Printed and bound in Dubai by Emirates Printing Press

FOREWORD

When I first met Liliane van der Hoeven at the Sheikh Mohammed Centre for Cultural Understanding (SMCCU) located in the historic Al Fahidi district, I was impressed to hear how she had taken up the challenge to create a children's book about our city and culture. When I read Liliane's manuscript it was clear that she not only had a genuine interest, but had made a great effort to truly understand our culture which is so different to her own. As an author, Liliane has succeeded in her quest to present our history, culture and heritage in an attractive and engaging way. Her colourful and lively illustrations will undoubtedly capture the interest and stimulate the imaginations of all the young people who will read *The Key to Dubai*.

Dubai is a truly cosmopolitan city, a popular travel destination and a home to families from all over the world. His Highness Sheikh Mohammed bin Rashid Al Maktoum, Vice President and Prime Minister of the UAE and Ruler of Dubai, saw the need to reach out and educate expatriates in the traditions and customs of the UAE. His vision led to the creation of SMCCU in 1998. *The Key to Dubai* supports our mission as it reaches out to children and their parents, many of whom will be experiencing our culture for the first time, and introduces them to our culture and history. Children have a wonderful desire to embrace the world around them, and this book is a compelling way to educate them about that world. I believe the key to tolerance and acceptance of one another is to learn about each other and *The Key to Dubai* does that. It will also prompt children to find out more and discover Dubai's most interesting places.

I hope that all the young readers will enjoy the journey while exploring the pages of *The Key to Dubai*. The motto of our centre is 'Open doors. Open minds', and so I invite you to visit us and experience the Emirati culture through the wide range of activities we offer.

I look forward to welcoming you to our centre.

Nasif Kayed
Managing Director, Sheikh Mohammed Centre for Cultural Understanding

THIS BOOK BELONGS TO:

_____

CONTENTS

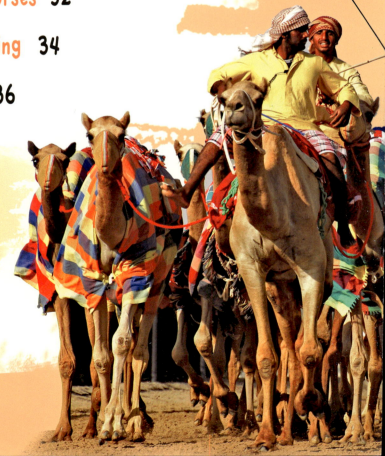

Look out for the small keys in the book for tips on where to go and what to do, so you can experience Dubai to the max!

MARHABA! WELCOME!

Welcome to Dubai, the famous city in the United Arab Emirates (UAE). Home to the world's tallest tower and an island in the shape of a palm tree, there is lots to discover about this fascinating place.

Looking at the city's impressive skyline, it is hard to imagine that Dubai was once just a small fishing village. How did it grow under its rulers into today's ultra-modern city? What was life like for Bedouins living in a hot and empty desert? Why are camels and falcons so important to Emirati people? And how do people dress? *The Key to Dubai* will show you Dubai, its people and the UAE's rich culture and traditions. Discover the whys and hows, as well as the key facts.

Look out for the small keys in the book for tips on where to go and what to do, so you can experience Dubai to the max!

HH SHEIKH KHALIFA BIN ZAYED AL NAHYAN

President of the UAE and Ruler of Abu Dhabi.

HH SHEIKH MOHAMMED BIN RASHID AL MAKTOUM

Vice President and Prime Minister of the UAE and Ruler of Dubai.

The United Arab Emirates is made up of seven emirates. Each emirate has its own ruler, called a sheikh. The country's president is Sheikh Khalifa, ruler of the largest emirate, Abu Dhabi.

A **MAJLIS** is a place to gather, drink coffee or entertain family and guests. A sheikh often receives guests in his majlis to discuss important matters and exchange ideas.

Guests are welcomed with Arabic **COFFEE** and fresh **DATES**.

IX

DUBAI IN THE

UAE

UNITED ARAB EMIRATES

Dubai is one of the seven emirates that make up the one nation, named the United Arab Emirates, also simply called the UAE or The Emirates. The seven emirates of the UAE are: Abu Dhabi, Dubai, Sharjah, Ajman, Umm Al Quwain, Ras Al Khaimah and Fujairah. The capital city is Abu Dhabi.

The weather in the UAE is mostly sunny. Sandstorms and rainfall happen just a few times a year. In the summer, the temperature rises to 45 degrees celsius and becomes very humid.

The falcon is the UAE's national symbol

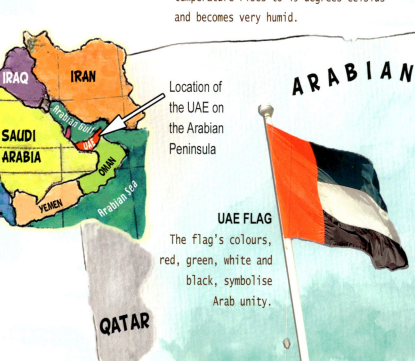

Location of the UAE on the Arabian Peninsula

LOCATION

The UAE is a country in the Middle East and situated along the Arabian Gulf. It shares borders with Saudi Arabia, Oman and Qatar. The UAE's land area is 83,600 square kilometres. Abu Dhabi is by far the largest emirate with 87% of the country's total area.

UAE FLAG

The flag's colours, red, green, white and black, symbolise Arab unity.

Sheikh Zayed bin Sultan Al Nahyan

RULERS

Each of the seven emirates is governed by a hereditary emir called a sheikh. The country has a single president. The first president, after the UAE was born on 2 December, 1971, was Sheikh Zayed bin Sultan Al Nahyan. He is still remembered as the 'Father of the Nation'.

Today's President of the UAE is Sheikh Zayed's son, Sheikh Khalifa bin Zayed Al Nahyan, the Ruler of Abu Dhabi. Dubai's Ruler, Sheikh Mohammed bin Rashid Al Maktoum, is also the UAE's Vice President and Prime Minister.

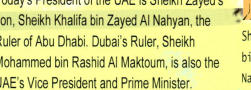

Sheikh Khalifa bin Zayed Al Nahyan

Sheikh Mohammed bin Rashid Al Maktoum

LANDSCAPE

Most of the UAE is desert land, but there are mountains, oases and beaches too. The most spectacular golden sand dunes are found in Liwa (Abu Dhabi) with dunes reaching up to 120m. The Hajar mountains have many wadis (dry river beds). Whenever it rains, they fill up quickly with water running down the mountains.

Liwa desert

wadi

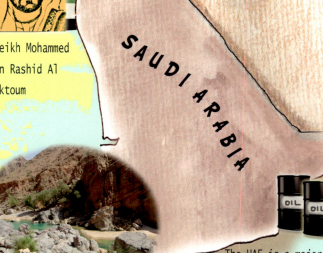

The UAE is a major producer and exporter of oil. Most of the oil is found in Abu Dhabi.

GULF

RAS AL KHAIMAH

UMM AL QUWAIN

AJMAN

SHARJAH

DUBAI

Dubai

FUJAIRAH

Hajar Mountains

ABU DHABI
Capital city

Al Ain

OMAN

Abu Dhabi

The UAE's largest
emirate occupies
87% of the country's
total area.

This map is not drawn to scale and it is not an authority on international
and administrative boundaries. It is for illustrative purposes only.

The seven emirates and their capitals
have the same name (eg. Dubai city is
located within the emirate of Dubai).

PEOPLE
The UAE has over nine million residents. About 15%
are locals, called Emiratis. Many expats from across
the globe have come to work and live in the UAE.

RELIGION
The official and largest religion in the UAE is Islam. Local people (Emiratis)
are Muslims and go to mosques for prayer. The many other nationalities
living in the country have various religious backgrounds.

ARABIC

welcome / hello	مرحبا
	marhaba
thank you	شكراً
	shukran
how are you?	كيف الحال
	kifal hal
goodbye	مع السلامة
	ma'assalama

0 = .
1 = ١
2 = ٢
3 = ٣
4 = ٤
5 = ٥
6 = ٦
7 = ٧
8 = ٨
9 = ٩

LANGUAGE
The UAE's official language
is Arabic. English is also
widely spoken. Arabic is
taught to every child in
school. The Arabic
language is written
from right to left.

MONEY
The currency of the UAE is the United
Arab Emirates Dirham (Dhs. or AED).
Have a closer look at the coins and
banknotes. They show various symbols
that are important to the country, such
as the falcon, Arabic coffee pot, gazelle,
oil derricks, dhow, and the date palm.

1 dirham

25 fils

50 fils

FROM PAST TO PRESENT

Knowing Dubai as it is today, it is difficult to imagine that this city was once only a small fishing village. How did it grow into this very modern and cosmopolitan city with a clear mark on the world map?
Dubai's story is an impressive one, from the vision of its rulers to the milestones of the past, present and future.

By 1930, Dubai has around 20,000 people, of which 25% are foreigners. The pearl industry starts to face difficult times. The global economy is struggling and Japan discovers a way to grow pearls artificially. Soon, Dubai's pearl trade collapses and many people lose their livelihoods.

THEN

1833

1900

1930

1959

Dredger, Creek 1959

Dubai Creek

Members of the Bani Yas Tribe leave the Liwa Oasis (Abu Dhabi) to look for a better place to live. They are led by the Al Maktoum family. When they arrive in Dubai – a small fishing village near the Arabian Gulf – they decide to settle down at the mouth of Dubai Creek (Shindagha). Ever since, Dubai has been under the rule of the Al Maktoum royal family.

Pearl diving, fishing and sea trade provide income for the people living along the coast. After 1894, Dubai's economy flourishes when Sheikh Maktoum offers zero tax charges to foreign traders. This makes Dubai a popular free trade port for the import and export of goods. As the region's centre for foreign trade, Dubai attracts traders and merchants from abroad to live and work in Dubai. Coral-stone windtower houses and warehouses appear on the banks of the creek. A large souk on the Deira side of the creek is the place to buy and sell goods.

In 1959, Sheikh Rashid who succeeded his father Sheikh Saeed, takes a crucial step for Dubai's future. He gives orders to dredge the creek that is becoming unaccessible for ships because of silting. The restored depth enables Dubai to grow into the largest trading and export centre of the Middle East.

Sheikh Rashid: the 'Founding Father of Modern Dubai' with his son Mohammed

4

In 1966, oil is discovered in Dubai. With money from the oil exports flowing in, Sheikh Rashid greatly improves the city's infrastructure. Roads, schools, hospitals and drainage are constructed as well as a new port (Port Rashid), accommodating the largest ships, a telecom network, and Dubai International Airport is also expanded.

1966

Dubai World Trade Centre, 1979

2010

Dubai and its free trade options attract companies from all over the world. In 1979, the World Trade Centre, Dubai's first skyscraper appears, with many other high-rise buildings to follow. Six years later, Dubai has its own airline, named Emirates.

Dubai 2015

1979

1971

UAE

tineline

NOW

In 1971, the United Arab Emirates (UAE) is officially born. Sheikh Zayed (Abu Dhabi) and Sheikh Rashid (Dubai) are the driving forces to unite the seven emirates – Abu Dhabi, Dubai, Sharjah, Ajman, Umm Al Quwain, Fujairah and Ras Al Khaimah – into one single state.

1999

Dubai aims to become a favourite tourist destination. In 1999, the prestigious Burj Al Arab, known as the world's most luxurious hotel, opens its doors. Under the rule of Sheikh Mohammed, Dubai's current leader, Vice President and Prime Minister of the UAE, other unique and world famous construction projects such as the Palm Jumeirah, The Dubai Mall and the Burj Khalifa, soon follow.

Every year since, the UAE celebrates its birthday on 2 December, called National Day.

At the **Dubai Museum** in Bur Dubai, you can make a journey through Dubai's history, from before the discovery of oil to the present day. The **Sheikh Saeed Al Maktoum House** in the Shindagha district shows historic photographs of Dubai. The building is the former house and government seat of the late Sheikh Saeed. Info: www.dubaiculture.gov.ae

EXPO 2020 DUBAI, UAE

FUTURE

In 2020, Dubai will host the World Expo. The pavilions will highlight future innovations and developments. Dubai aims to increase the number of visitors to the emirate to 20 million by 2020.

DUBAI, THE CITY

The city of Dubai is located within the emirate of the same name. This ultra-modern and dynamic city has seen amazing growth in the last 50 years. Most of the emirate's 2.3 million people live and work here. Daily, an extra one million travel into the city for work, a visit or holiday. Dubai offers them various modern modes of public transport to move around.

kyline

WORLD RECORD!

tallest

THE RISE OF DUBAI

As Dubai grew over time, so did its buildings. For almost 200 years the Al Fahidi Fort was Dubai's tallest structure. After the construction of the first skyscraper – Dubai World Trade Centre's Sheikh Rashid Tower – many taller ones followed. The famous Burj Khalifa tower, at 828m high, set the new world record.

Burj Khalifa
828m

1991

THEN & NOW

2015

AMAZING GROWTH

Dubai developed rapidly, soon after oil was discovered in the emirate (1966). Money from oil exports was used to improve the city's infrastructure which enabled Dubai to grow into the ultra-modern city we know today.

taller

Dubai World Trade Centre
149m

tall

Al Fahidi Fort
12.5m

Emirates

6

1787   1979   2010

A huge portrait of the late Sheikh Zayed along the highway that carries his name.

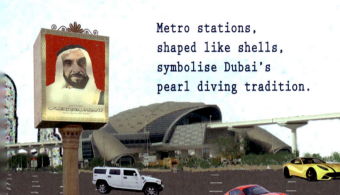

Metro stations, shaped like shells, symbolise Dubai's pearl diving tradition.

The Dubai Metro is the longest, driverless metro network in the world (74km).

SHEIKH ZAYED ROAD

Dubai's main highway is named after the late Sheikh Zayed, the first president of the UAE. The road is seven lanes wide and runs parallel to the coastline of the Arabian Gulf. It is part of the E11 – the longest road in the UAE that connects Dubai to Abu Dhabi. At the other end, the E11 stretches all the way to the Oman border.

AIRPORT

Dubai International Airport (DXB) is the busiest airport in the world with over 70 million passengers passing through in 2014. Dubai's own airline, Emirates, is based at Terminal 3.

EMIRATES AIRLINE

In 1985, Emirates started flying from Dubai with only two aeroplanes. Today, its fleet has over 220 aircraft and more double-decker planes than anywhere else in the world.

This giant, new airport building with 20 gates was especially designed for the double-decker A380 superjumbos in Dubai.

GETTING IN & AROUND

Dubai	60 km
Al Sharjah	77 km
Ajman	91 km
Umm Al Quwain	109 km
Ras Al Khaimah	152 km
Al Fujeirah	190 km

The A380 can carry 644 passengers

GETTING AROUND

Many luxury cars cruise down Dubai's roads. There are plenty of taxis available. The ones with pink rooftops are called Ladies' Taxis. They have female drivers that only take women and families on board. People do not only get around by car, new and advanced bus, metro and tram services are also available.

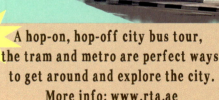

Dubai Tram

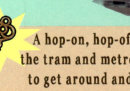

An air-conditioned bus stop

A hop-on, hop-off city bus tour, the tram and metro are perfect ways to get around and explore the city. More info: www.rta.ae

KEY FACTS

Did you know? Emirates Airline ...

... flies more than 44 million passengers per year to over 140 destinations around the world

... owns the most Airbus A380s and Boeing 777 aeroplanes

... has over 1,500 flights from Dubai each week

... is using a special terminal – the first of its kind – just for its A380s

... has won many international awards

SKYLINE

In only 10 years, Dubai's skyline became one of the largest in the world. Many buildings are fine examples of modern architecture with shapes that are truly fascinating.

TOWERS

Most of the high-rise buildings that dominate Dubai's skyline appeared over the last 10 years. They provide homes, office space and hotel accommodation. Now the city is home to over 250 buildings that are at least 100m (328ft) tall, and more are underway.

INTERESTING SHAPES

Architects gave many of the city's new buildings very innovative designs. Have a look at some interesting shapes from different areas across the city.

CONSTRUCTION AHEAD !

A lot of construction work takes place throughout the city

عمال يشتغلون
MEN AT WORK

حفريات عميقة
Deep Excavation

1. Emirates Towers
2. DIFC - The Gate
3. Chelsea Tower
4. Dusit Thani Hotel
5. Etisalat Tower 2
6. 23 Marina
7. Index Tower
8. Burj Dubai Lake Hotel
9. Jumeirah Beach Hotel
10. Cayan Tower

HAVE YOU SPOTTED THESE 10 YET?

1.
2.
3.
4.
5.
6.
7.
8.

The tower with a 90-degree twist.

10.
9.

Cleaning skyscrapers' windows takes time and courage

8

Jumeirah Lakes Towers (JLT) is home to many office buildings.

Sheikh Zayed Road

Only 15 years ago you would have found empty desert here!

INCREDIBLE GROWTH

Dubai's first skyscrapers appeared along the Sheikh Zayed Road. Soon after, big construction projects in other areas started. Together they create an amazing skyline.

Dubai Marina has a man-made marina. A walkway (the Marina Walk) takes you past the yachts and waterfront restaurants.

Jumeirah Beach Residence (JBR) has a beachfront boulevard (The Walk) with shops and restaurants. In front of JBR is 'The Beach'. This complex offers various attractions like an outdoor cinema and water parks.

FAMOUS LANDMARKS

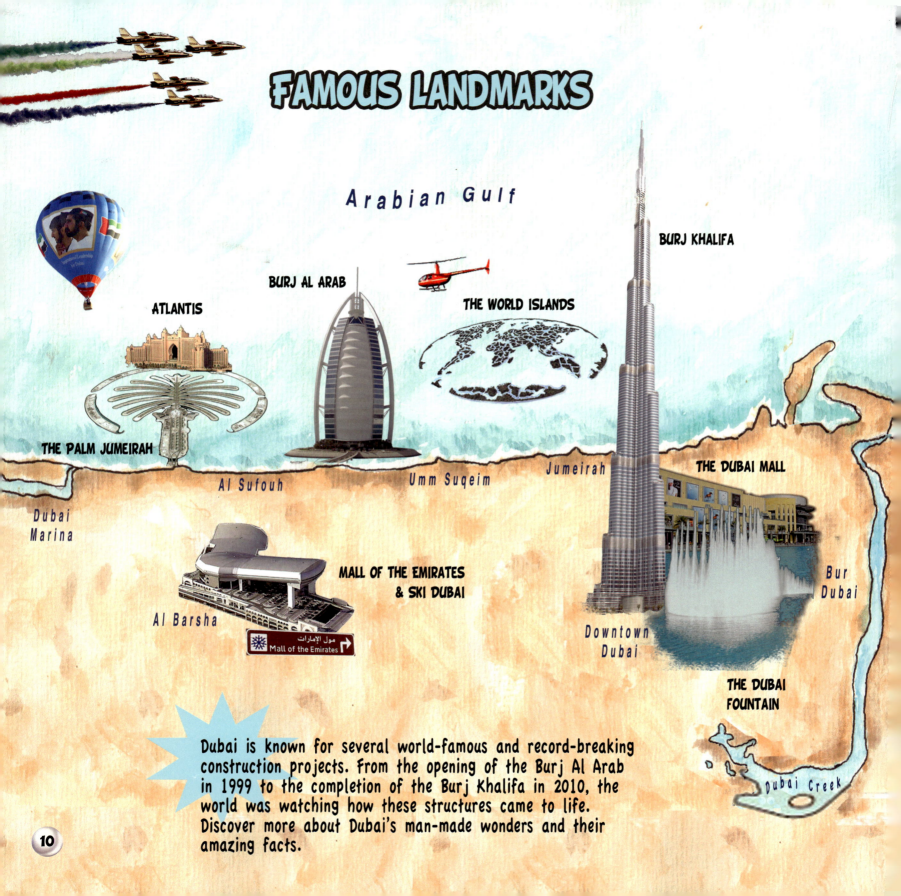

Arabian Gulf

BURJ KHALIFA

BURJ AL ARAB

THE WORLD ISLANDS

ATLANTIS

THE PALM JUMEIRAH

Al Sufouh

Umm Suqeim

Jumeirah

THE DUBAI MALL

Dubai Marina

MALL OF THE EMIRATES & SKI DUBAI

Al Barsha

مول الإمارات
Mall of the Emirates ➤

Downtown Dubai

Bur Dubai

THE DUBAI FOUNTAIN

Dubai Creek

Dubai is known for several world-famous and record-breaking construction projects. From the opening of the Burj Al Arab in 1999 to the completion of the Burj Khalifa in 2010, the world was watching how these structures came to life. Discover more about Dubai's man-made wonders and their amazing facts.

BURJ AL ARAB 1999

meaning 'The tower of the Arabs', was designed to become the icon of Dubai, just like the Eiffel Tower is for Paris. Shaped like a giant billowing sail of an Arabian dhow (boat), it represents Dubai's historical connection with the sea. It is famous for being the most luxurious hotel in the world, and took five years to complete.

At night, a colourful light show is frequently projected onto the unique fabric-coated fibreglass screen of the 'sail'.

3.21m tall!
Higher than the Eiffel Tower!

helipad

In 2005, Andre Agassi and Roger Federer played tennis on the Burj Al Arab's helipad 212m (695ft) above the sea. The 20-minute match took place on a specially laid tennis court.

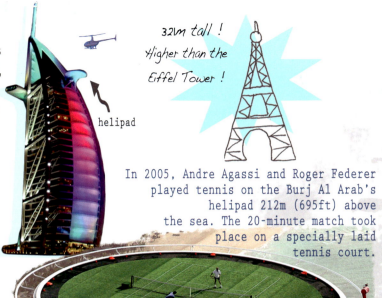

SKI DUBAI 2005

located inside the Mall of the Emirates is the world's largest indoor snow park. Don't let the desert stop you from going skiing, snowboarding or sledging in real, fresh snow. There are even penguins around!

KEY FACTS

Did you know? Ski Dubai...

... has five different slopes, up to 400m long

... offers the world's first indoor black run

... is the first indoor ski centre in the Middle East

tallest

largest

A dredger from the Dutch company Van Oord pumping sand (rainbowing) onto The Palm Jumeirah.

THE PALM JUMEIRAH 2007

is the world's largest man-made island. Built in the shape of a palm tree, it has a 2km long trunk, 17 fronds and a surrounding crescent.

As much as 40 million truck loads of sand!

The palm-shape is most visible from the sky.

Construction of beachfront villas on the fronds

How was The Palm Jumeirah constructed?
First, the crescent-shaped breakwater was made from massive rocks. Then, dredgers sprayed sand – taken from the sea floor further off the coast – to create land in water. GPS navigation and satellite pictures helped to construct the island into the exact shape of a palm tree.

KEY FACTS

Did you know? The Palm Jumeirah ....

... used 94 million cubic metres of sand and 5.5 million cubic metres of rock

... is 5km wide and 5km long

... can be seen from the moon with the naked eye

... created 78km of extra beachfront

... has a crescent to break the waves of the sea

... contains 4,000 houses and apartments that were sold within 72 hours in 2007

ATLANTIS 2008

proudly stands at the end of The Palm Jumeirah. The hotel resort has an underwater theme. It includes the Lost Chambers Aquarium, the Aquaventure water park and a chance to swim with dolphins. A huge firework show at its grand opening had the world watching.

2008
THE DUBAI MALL

is the largest shopping and entertainment destination in the world and is located next to the Burj Khalifa tower. A true paradise for shopping fans. Besides shopping, you can dine, watch movies, fly an Emirates A380, skate at the ice rink, visit the massive aquarium, or play games at Sega World. Don't get lost in this huge mall!

Dubai Aquarium & Underwater Zoo has more than 33,000 marine animals

floor space = **200** football pitches!

The Dubai Mall

2008
THE WORLD ISLANDS

is a group of 300 artificial islands. Together they form a map of the world. The continents lie 4km off the coast of Dubai. Construction on top of the islands is underway.

Dubai Ice Rink's olympic-size skating area

KEY FACTS

Did you know? The Dubai Mall ...

... covers 5.9 million square feet of floor space

... houses around 160 places to eat and drink

... has an aquarium with the world's largest viewing panel and a tunnel so you can walk under the fish

... offers 14,000 parking spaces

... attracts over 75 million visitors each year

2009
THE DUBAI FOUNTAIN

is the largest dancing fountain in the world. Situated in the Burj Lake, it shoots water from five circles up to 500ft (150m) in the air. This performance is accompanied by music and an impressive light show thanks to 6,600 superlights and 25 colour projectors. The fountain 'dances' daily to various songs and is a great spectacle to watch.

Shoots up to 150m high !

828m !
The world's **tallest** building.

2010
BURJ KHALIFA

with its 828m (2,716ft) height, is the tallest structure on Earth. The tower was named after the UAE's President, Sheikh Khalifa.

It took 22 million man-hours, over six years, to build the tower. At the peak of construction there were over 12,000 people working on site every day.

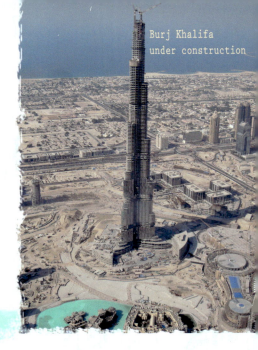

Burj Khalifa under construction

Travel at **10m/s** to the 124th floor observation deck in an elevator

The world's highest outdoor observation deck lies at 555m (1,820ft). With clear skies, you can see the Palm and World islands!

DESIGN
For the design, the architect Adrian Smith was inspired by a regional desert flower. You can recognise the stem and the petals. The shape reduces wind forces on the tower and maximises views from the windows.

the Hymenocallis flower

top view Burj Khalifa

More than **24,000** windows! It takes up to four months to clean them all.

Burj Khalifa houses luxury apartments, a hotel, restaurants and offices.

KEY FACTS
Did you know? Burj Khalifa ...

... is visible 95km (60 miles) away if skies are clear
... sways about 1.5m (5ft) at the top
... is built on 192 piles, going over 50m (164ft) deep
... used 330,000m³ of concrete and 39,000 tonnes of reinforced steel
... has double-deck elevators with the world's longest travel distance. In their five years of duty they travelled the distance from Earth to the moon (384,400km)

Book a visit to the **Burj Khalifa At the Top observation decks** for magnificent views of the city, sea and desert. Info: www.burjkhalifa.ae

13

PEOLE

TAILOR
خياط

The emirate of Dubai has the UAE's largest population. Less than 10% of the 2.3 million people in Dubai are locals.

EMIRATIS

Local people of the United Arab Emirates are called Emiratis. They make up less than 15% of the nine million UAE residents. Locals speak Arabic and most of them also English. Since the UAE is a Muslim country, local people go to mosques for prayer. For Emiratis, family is very important. Often large families live together in one house. The house has a living room to receive guests (majlis), often separated for men and women.

MORE THAN 200 NATIONALITIES!

Dubai attracts people from across the world (expats) who come to work in this fast-growing city. There are more than 200 different nationalities here, mostly from countries in South Asia, the Arab region, the US and Europe. No wonder that besides Arabic you can hear many other languages, like English, Urdu, Hindi or Tagalog in Dubai.

Although Islam is the UAE's official religion, foreigners are free to practise their own. In this multicultural and diverse society, you will find restaurants serving food from around the world and many international schools.

Most people work from Sunday until Thursday and enjoy the weekend on Fridays and Saturdays.

A sign often seen at the entrance to malls or other public places.

Please wear conservative clothing

We advise avoiding showing your shoulders and knees.

BIN and BINT

Arab names, as shown on some street signs, often use the word *bin* or *bint*. *Bin* means '*son of*' and *bint* '*daughter of*'.
Let's look at the name of the Ruler of Dubai: Sheikh Mohammed bin Rashid Al Maktoum means that the Sheikh is the son of Rashid, and Al Maktoum is his family name.
Female names also include their father's name. This does not change when a woman gets married.

Rubbing noses as a way of greeting shows friendship and deep respect.

DOS AND DON'TS

Emirati people are very friendly and welcoming to foreigners. It is important to respect their culture and local customs. What you should know...

Photography
Ask permission before you take pictures of local people, especially women.

Clothing
Wear modest clothing when you visit a public place or conservative area. Swimwear is only acceptable at the beach or around the pool.

Greetings
Handshakes are common but not every woman appreciates one from a man. Better to check to see if she offers her hand first. Sometimes men greet each other by rubbing noses. This is a local custom, only used between close friends as a sign of deep respect.

Public Displays of Affection
Emiratis don't show affection in public and they don't appreciate it when others do. **15**

EMIRATI DRESS

The national dress in the UAE is a long and loose robe combined with a headscarf. This style suits the country's climate as it protects the body from the hot sun and sand blowing around. Today, men are mostly dressed in white and women in black.

FOR MEN

The Emirati dress for men is a white, long dress (kandoura) combined with a headscarf (ghutra). The scarf is traditionally white. The red and white checked version is more casual and is also common in the UAE. The ghutra is worn in different ways. The ends either hang down or are thrown on the opposite shoulder. Another way is to tie both ends at the back. This style is often worn in the desert and is popular among young Emiratis.

BISHT
Loose robe usually black or beige with golden embroidery. It is worn over the kandoura on special occasions like weddings or official events.

KANDOURA
The everyday dress for Emirati men is the long and collarless shirt, called a kandoura or thawb. The colour white is most common, but in winter time, 'warmer' colours such as beige, blue or brown are also popular.

GHAFIYAH
A white knitted cap worn under the ghutra.

AGAL
The black cord was originally used to tie the camel's front legs so it would not stray.

white ghutra with black agal

kandoura

GHUTRA
This square scarf is made of cotton or silk. A black cord (agal) keeps the ghutra in place.

TARBOUSH
The tassel hanging from the neckline is for decoration, just like a tie. Before, men used to soak it in perfume so it would give off a nice smell wherever they went.

16

FOR WOMEN

Emirati women wear long and loose black clothing. It covers the body, hair and sometimes the face. For them, covering up is part of Muslim life. The colour black has become part of Emirati culture.

WHY BLACK?

In the past, abayas had various colours. Why did it become black? Some say the colour got popular after a famous poem about an elegant lady in black. Other stories tell there was once a tailor who ordered too much black fabric and black became the only colour available. Although black seems to be the wrong colour to wear in a hot climate, Emirati women will reassure you that the abaya is airy and comfortable, thanks to its loose fit and lightweight fabric. Black is also perfect to conceal the trendy outfits worn underneath.

Today, the abaya is a fashion statement for many Emirati girls and women. You will see nicely tailored abayas with beautiful embroidery, shiny beads, gems or crystals, both on the street and the catwalk.

FASHION

Trendy and elegant abayas designed by Emirati fashion designer Amal Murad
Photos: REDAA
Dubai Fashion Week

sheila

abaya

SHEILA
A large piece of black fabric that covers a woman's head and hair.

ABAYA
The long, black dress is worn for modesty on top of women's clothes. Whenever women go to public places or find themselves in the company of men other than family members, they will put on their abayas and sheilas.

FACE COVERING

burqa

One of the oldest items of Emirati dress is the face mask (burqa). It covers the entire face except the eyes and is nowadays mostly worn by older women. Some people think it is made of metal, but it is not. Originally, the burqa was made from leather to protect the face from the sun and sand. The inside was dyed with indigo to beautify the skin. The outside was often painted with a gold colour.

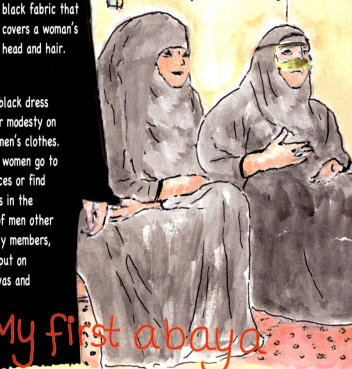

My first abaya

"I used to have it there between all my dressing up costumes in my dress up box. Whenever I would pretend play I was a mother, I would put on my abaya and pretend I was all grown up. I would always dream of the day I would be old enough to wear one. Until the day came where I decided it was time. It made me feel so good to wear my abaya, my pretty black abaya with sparkly crystals on. I loved wearing it, because it made me feel secure about myself at a stage in life where I was insecure about the clothes and outfits I would wear."

-Amani Abdulla

17

RELIGION

You can see and hear many mosques in Dubai. This is because the UAE is a Muslim country. Emiratis and many foreign people living here are Muslim. They follow the religion of Islam. Muslims pray to Allah (God) and the Quran is their holy book. It contains the word of Allah, as told to the Prophet Mohammad.

MECCA

When Muslims pray they always face in the direction of Mecca. Mecca is a city in Saudi Arabia and the birthplace of Prophet Mohammad. To Muslims, this is the holiest place on Earth. Every Muslim family knows the direction from their house to Mecca.

In hotel rooms you'll often find an arrow on the ceiling pointing towards Mecca.

Muslims try to visit Mecca at least once in their life. That's why every year millions of Muslims from around the world make a pilgrimage to Mecca (Hajj).

Sheikh Zayed Grand Mosque in Abu Dhabi

THE FIVE PILLARS OF ISLAM show people how to lead a Muslim life. These are:

Belief that there is only one God (Allah)
Prayer five times a day
Giving 2.5% of your yearly savings to charity
Fasting during the month of Ramadan
Making a journey to Mecca at least once in your lifetime.

I S L A M
5

RAMADAN

Ramadan is the holy month of fasting. All Muslim adults and children past the age of puberty will not eat or drink during daylight hours. It is a way to purify themselves, gain self-control and focus on God through prayer.

Jumeirah Mosque in Dubai

Each evening after sunset, Muslims break their fast by eating fresh dates, followed by a festive dinner. This is called the Iftar Feast.

During Ramadan it is prohibited to eat or drink in public before sunset. Everyone, including tourists and non-Muslims, should be discreet about it to show respect to the local culture.

How Do Muslims Pray?

Muslims pray five times a day. When the call to prayer is heard, men go to the nearest mosque. Most women pray at home. There are also prayer rooms available in offices and shopping malls.

Friday is a special day for prayer. On this day, many Muslims visit the mosque to listen to the sermon from the Imam — the man who leads the prayers. As women do not pray with men, you'll find a separate prayer area for women.

Before prayer, Muslims first wash their hands, mouth, nose, face, arms to elbows, and feet to ankles. Before entering the mosque or prayer room people take off their shoes. Then they start praying on a prayer mat facing the direction of Mecca.

Would you like to visit a mosque or know more about the religion of Islam? The Sheikh Mohammed Centre for Cultural Understanding offers tours for non-Muslims in Dubai's famous Jumeirah Mosque. To enter the mosque, you must cover your arms, shoulders and knees. Women should also cover their heads. Info: www.cultures.ae

MOSQUE

Every neighbourhood has a mosque. It is the House of Allah and a place of prayer for Muslims. A mosque has one or more domes and minarets on its roof, often beautifully decorated.

You can hear the voice of the man (muezzin) calling Muslims to prayer through the speakers of the minaret. The taller the minaret, the further the call (adhaan), five times a day, will be heard.

Mosque = 'masjid' in Arabic

MINARET

DOME

QUIBLA
The wall in a mosque facing Mecca.

PRAYER TIMES

QURAN

MIHRAB
Every mosque has this niche in the wall that serves as a passage to Mecca. It shows the direction one should face while praying.

Shoes off before you enter

TRADITIONS

The UAE has a rich Arab culture, showing a strong influence of the religion of Islam and Bedouin life. The first things you will notice when you visit the UAE are the hospitality and national dress of the Emirati people. These and many other traditions are highlighted in this book.

ARABIC COFFEE

Serving home-prepared Arabic coffee (gahwah) to guests is an important part of Arab hospitality. Beans are first roasted in a pan, then ground and brewed in a clay pot. Some cardamom, saffron or rosewater is added to flavour the coffee. When serving guests, the coffee is poured from a 'dallah' (pot with beak), held in the left hand, into small ceramic cups, held in the right hand. The host will keep refilling your cup, until you indicate you have had enough by shaking the cup slightly from side to side.

Arabic coffee is often served with dates

'Tawa':
roasting pan for coffee beans

'Dallah':
the traditional coffee pot

Cardamom

Saffron

FOOD

Dubai today has food, dishes and restaurants from all over the world, but traditional Emirati cuisine still exists. Home-cooked meals often include fish, meat, rice, wheat and dairy. Dishes are often stews cooked in a single pot and flavoured with spices such as saffron, turmeric, thyme and cardamom. Muslims only eat 'halal' food, which means that it is allowed to be eaten according to Islamic law.

'Gaimat':
crunchy dough balls with date molasses

NO PORK! Muslims do not eat pork. Some supermarkets have separate sections to sell pork products to non-Muslims.

Join a traditional Emirati meal at the Sheikh Mohammed Centre for Cultural Understanding in the historic Al Fahidi district (Bastakiya) or visit the Heritage Village in Shindagha to learn more about Emirati life. Info: www.dubaiculture.gov.ae

HENNA

Traditional henna painting is mostly used by women to decorate their hands and feet and to dye their hair. It is still popular with locals and visitors to Dubai.

Emirati women use henna as make-up for celebrations, such as weddings. The henna dye comes from the henna tree. Its leaves are dried, ground to powder, and then mixed with lime and hot water to form a thick paste. When applied to your skin the paste will dye it with an orange/brown colour. Henna artists can draw beautiful patterns, including floral designs. A henna tattoo is painless and will last for about a week; a nice souvenir for tourists to take home!

HOSPITALITY

Bedouins in the desert lived by the rule that every stranger arriving at the camp should be offered food and shelter for at least three days.

Na'ashat dance

MUSIC AND DANCE

Story-telling, poetry, songs and dance are part of the UAE's folklore. Different songs were composed for different tasks in life, such as hauling water or rowing the pearling boat. Traditional dances are often performed at weddings, sporting events and national festivals.

Ayyala dance

NA'ASHAT DANCE

Young women in bright, traditional dress stand in a line and show the beauty of their long hair by swaying it from side to side.

AYYALA DANCE

In this energetic war dance, men drum, sing and dance with sticks, rifles or swords.

21

IN THE DESERT

BEDOUIN LIFE

Bedouins are nomadic people who live in the desert. They move from oasis to oasis. A tent is their home.

When Bedouins settle down for a longer time, they build houses by using various parts of the palm tree.

DATE PALMS grow in oases. The trees not only provide dates but also materials to make houses and various household items.

Bedouins herd **CAMELS**, **SHEEP** and **GOATS.** The animals provide milk, wool and meat to the family. The products are also sold at local markets.

CAMELS are mainly used for milk and transportation. Their meat is only served on special occasions like weddings.

Today, it is hard to find people that still live a true Bedouin life in Dubai. Many locals come from Bedouin families and still combine the old traditions with today's modern lifestyle.

Wild **FALCONS** are captured and trained to hunt for food.

Desert life thrives in winter when animals graze and crops grow. Before summer arrives there is leisure time for hunting and camel racing. During the hot summer months people settle down in oases or move to coastal areas.

TENTS are made of woven goat and camel hair.

Women take care of livestock or engage in **CRAFTS** such as spinning wool from goat hair, pottery or weaving palm leaves into baskets or mats.

HOSPITALITY is important to Bedouins. Arabic coffee is always ready to be served.

The slender **SALUKI** dog is a very fast hunter.

Owning an **ARABIAN HORSE** is very precious. It is kept near, or even inside, the owner's tent.

CAMELS

The Arabian camel (or dromedary) has only one hump. It is a unique mammal that has adapted perfectly to life in the desert. To Bedouins, the camel is a 'gift of God', because it supports them in so many ways.

As 'ships of the desert', camels can travel long distances while carrying people and heavy freight. The camel was also used for trade, in fighting other tribes, or for having fun by racing them. It is also a source of milk and meat. Hair and hide are used to make items such as tents, clothes, rugs, bags, and saddles.

Double row eyelashes and hair inside the ears keep dust and sand out

Nostrils can be closed in sand storms

It can smell water from 2km away

Thick, rubbery lips for eating thorny desert plants

HOW DO CAMELS SURVIVE IN THE DESERT?

The hump contains fat for extra energy when food is scarce. It will collapse if the camel goes hungry for a long time

Camels are champions in conserving water. As their body temperature adapts to the heat, they don't lose water through sweating.

Rough pads on the knees for sitting on the hot sand

Camels sway as they move both legs on one side of the body at the same time.

The broad feet with two toes do not sink in the soft sand.

Camel = 'jamal' in Arabic

A camel's teeth can tell its age

Find out more about this unique desert animal at Dubai's Camel Museum. See: www.dubaiculture.ae

26

CAMEL MARKET

Camels in the UAE are still traded for their milk, meat and hides, or for breeding and racing. Trading takes place at a camel market or souk.

The price of a camel can vary between a few thousand and one million dirhams, especially if it involves a prize-winning race camel.

Camel souk

WATER

A thirsty camel can drink around **100 litres** (26 gallons) of water at a time. In summer, camels can go without drinking for two to four weeks, depending on the heat.

100 X 1Litre

During the winter, camels can survive up to three months without drinking, because they can consume water from plants.

Camels were once the only means of transport for Bedouins. Cars nowadays have taken over!

CAMEL FEED

A female camel carries her young for about 13 months. The baby camel can run straight after birth.

KEY CAMEL FACTS

Did you know?
... camels can be over 7ft (2.1m) tall and weigh over 500kg
... will spit when distressed or during mating season
... live up to 30-40 years
... can carry loads of up to 300kg
... camel poo is so dry that it can be used as fuel for a fire
... there are camel beauty contests in the UAE

CHOCOLATE camel milk

Camel milk is popular in the UAE. It is healthy, nutritious and sold in many supermarkets.

camel milk

27

DATE PALMS

The date palm was so important to Bedouins living in the desert that they named it 'the tree of life'.
It gave them shade from the desert sun, protection from desert winds, and dates to eat or bring along on long journeys through the desert.

An oasis with palm trees was the perfect place for Bedouins to settle down for a while. Palm trees provided various materials to make houses, fences and utensils.

DATES

The fruit of the palm tree is a symbol of Arab hospitality. Dates are offered to guests along with a cup of Arabic coffee or tea. The sweet and very nutritious dates are used in many Emirati dishes. During Ramadan, people eat dates after sunset to break the fast.

Dates grow in bunches. As they ripen, they turn from green to yellow to reddish orange. August to September is harvesting season.

WHAT WERE THE DIFFERENT PARTS OF THE DATE PALM USED FOR?

Palm tree trunks support the roof and corners of the house.

Leaves were dried and tied together to make a barasti for shades, roofs and enclosures.

Fronds were woven to make walls.

DATES

to make syrup, vinegar, cakes, and bread for the family and to feed animals.

Elastic fibres that cover the trunk were used to make saddles, ropes and fishing nets.

BARASTI HOUSE

HOUSEHOLD ITEMS

Palm leaves were also used to make mats and baskets. The leaf strips were first soaked in water to make them flexible enough for weaving.

Did you know?
Date production is the largest fruit farming industry in the UAE.

HOW TO CLIMB A PALM TREE?

In a few seconds this man climbs up the tree simply by using a rope.

KEY DATE PALM FACTS

Did you know ?
... dates only grow on female trees
... date palms live more than 200 years
... they grow from shoots
... a tree can grow 30m (100ft) tall
... trees need 70 litres of water every second day
... the roots go deep and far to seek water
... one tree can produce up to 230 kg
   of dates per year

FALAJ

This channel is part of a traditional irrigation system called 'falaj'. It transports water to the palm trees. The water flows from higher to lower parts of the plantation. The direction of the flow can be changed by blocking exits.

Falaj

FALCONS

These majestic birds of prey have always been important to the people of Dubai and the UAE. Many Bedouins still have a falcon at home, as a member of their family. The old tradition of falconry – training falcons and hunting with them – is still popular in the UAE.

IN THE PAST...

Bedouin people would capture wild falcons that flew over in autumn on their way to Africa (migration). The Bedouins started training these falcons for hunting animals such as wild rabbits, hares and the Houbara bustard. The prey caught by the falcons provided families with variety in the meat they ate.

Tribal sheikhs often took their falcons on hunting trips. This was a perfect way to connect with people living in remote areas of the desert. After a day of hunting the sheikh would sit down in a tent or around a campfire. People from the area were welcome to meet him to discuss things that were important to them.

Sheikh Zayed bin Sultan Al Nahyan holding a Peregrine falcon

TODAY...

Hunting with falcons is no longer allowed in the UAE. Falconry is practised as part of the Emirati lifestyle with training on artificial prey. Falcons kept at home come from breeding centres. Wild falcons are released into the wild to protect the population.

While resting, the falcon is tethered to a perch covered with artificial grass.

FALCON TRAINING

A bundle of feathers or a piece of raw meat lures the falcon during training sessions.

A falconer spends a lot of time with his falcon for bonding, taming and training. He gives it a name and keeps calling the bird so it will learn to recognise his voice. The leather hood (burqa) helps to tame the bird as it calms him down.

FALCONS IN THE UAE

SAKER FALCON
the most beautiful and the national bird of the UAE

GYR FALCON
the largest falcon in the UAE

PEREGRINE FALCON
the world's fastest flying bird

TOP SPEED 350KM/H !!!

3 FALCON SEASONS

SPRING

BREEDING 2-4 eggs per year

SUMMER

MOLTING new feathers

HUNTING

WINTER

FALCON'S PREY

Houbara bustard

Hare

KEY FALCON FACTS

Did you know?
... each falcon kept in the UAE has a passport
... its maximum age is 20 years
... females are 1/3 taller than males
... falcons change feathers every year
... a falcon costs between 5,000 and half a million Dhs.
... the large Gyr falcon can have a 1.2m wing span
... 85% of the falcons used for hunting are females
... they can carry up to six times their own weight
... falcons are very intelligent
... they have different personalities
... their eyes are six times stronger than the human eye
... they breathe through a hole in their tongues
... falcons only eat fresh meat and bones
... they originally lived in mountains, near to rivers and lakes

ABU DHABI FALCON HOSPITAL

EXAMINATION ROOM

PEDICURE

The largest falcon hospital in the world has a unique knowledge of falcons.

Falcons are brought in for health check ups or treatment for injuries like a broken wing. During the hunting season (winter time), the hospital sees around 140 falcons per day!

Would you like to see some falcons and learn more about them?

Visit the Abu Dhabi Falcon Hospital and join a guided tour. Info: www.falconhospital.com. Or, have a look at the Falcon Museum inside the Falcon Heritage and Sports Centre in Dubai. Info: www.dm.gov.ae

Special thanks to the Abu Dhabi Falcon Hospital

ARABIAN HORSES

For centuries, Arabian horses lived in the desert together with Bedouin families. A horse was considered to be a precious gift from God. For shelter and protection from theft, it was sometimes kept in the owner's tent. Arabians can travel long distances. They were used for transportation, breeding, trade, hunting and for fighting other tribes.

Arabian horses have a ⬤ bay, ⬤ grey, ⬤ chestnut, ⬤ black or ⬤ roan coat colour. Bay is the most common colour, black is somewhat rare. All Arabians have black skin underneath their coats for protection from the hot desert sun.

Arabian horses are pricey. For identification purposes, every horse has a passport and is branded with an iron.

Al Khamsa

Legend of the Five Mares
An old Bedouin belief says that a true Arabian horse can be traced back to *Al Khamsa* – the famous five mares. After a long journey in the desert, Prophet Mohammad turned his thirsty herd loose near an oasis. Before the horses reached the water to drink, Prophet Mohammad called them back. Only five mares faithfully responded and returned to him. They became his five favourite mares.

Horse = 'hisaan' in Arabic

DUBAI WORLD CUP

Horse racing is very popular in the UAE. The prestigious Dubai World Cup is the emirate's biggest sporting event, usually held in March at the Meydan Racecourse. It is the richest horse race in the world. Arabians, thoroughbreds and their jockeys race to win more than $20 million in prize money.

Sheikh Mohammed and his family share a passion for horse racing. Their own family racing stable Godolphin is very successful.

Frankie Dettori
Dubai World Cup
2010

tail carried high

strong chest

Visit the Horse Museum in Shindagha to find out more about horses and their importance to the Emirati people.
Info: www.dubaiculture.gov.ae

Sheikh Mohammed during a race in Dubai (2010).

ENDURANCE RACING

Arabian horses can race long distances due to their strong, muscular bodies and large lung capacities. Endurance racing is a popular sport in the UAE. Sheikh Mohammed, the Ruler of Dubai himself, became the endurance world champion in 2012.

In endurance racing, riders compete to set the best time in finishing a course laid out on desert terrain. A race can be up to 160km long and takes place over several loops. A rider must complete the course on one single horse. After each loop, the horse has time to rest and is inspected by a vet to ensure its wellbeing.

Sheikh Mohammed and his son, Crown Prince Hamdan, celebrate their victory (2009).

arched neck

curved ears

broad forehead

dished profile

big nostrils

short back

strong legs

FEATURES

Arabian horses are the 'purest' of all horse breeds. They have always been carefully bred by the Bedouins. Arabians look quite different from other horses due to their distinguished features. Even their skeletons are different; unlike other breeds, Arabians have 17 sets of ribs, not 18 sets.

CAMEL RACING

Running camels at speed over a course is one of the oldest sports in the UAE. It has always been part of Bedouin life and today is very popular amongst local people and royal families. Official races and training sessions take place in winter, from October to March, at various race tracks, also in Dubai.

**TOP SPEED
40MPH (65KM/H)**

Dromedary comes from the Greek word 'dromeus', which means 'runner'

RACE CAMELS

The dromedary or one-humped Arabian camel is known for its speed, reaching up to 65km/h. Its lighter skeleton makes it a better racer than the two-humped (Bactrian) camel.

Race camels start their training around three years of age. They are first tamed and will learn to walk long distances before they start training on a race course. A special diet keeps them healthy and strong. Most racers are female as they tend to run faster. There are separate races for males and females, and for different age groups.

Watching camels race is a real cultural treat! Visit the Dubai Camel Racing Festival, held in April at the Al Marmoum Race Track. Or, drive by in the early morning between October and March and you might be lucky to see camels in training!

Race distances on the oval-shaped track vary from 4km to 10km.

Al Marmoum Race Track
Al Ain Road (E66), Exit 37

The race champion is smeared with orange saffron.

Traditional camel racing

The number on the camel's neck indicates what race it will run.

Race champions can be worth a few million dirhams!

A **ROBOT JOCKEY** is tied onto a camel's back. The attached whip is run by a small motor. Towards the finish line, owners and trainers encourage their camels to run faster by using the robot's remote control while driving in their 4x4 cars alongside the track.

JOCKEYS

Traditionally, young men raced camels sitting behind the hump on the camel's back. The use of children is no longer allowed. Nowadays, human jockeys are often replaced by robotic jockeys, weighing less than seven pounds.

Robot Jockey

As robots don't tell camels to slow down, you will see trainers running after them once they have crossed the finish line.

Camels race with remote control robot jockeys

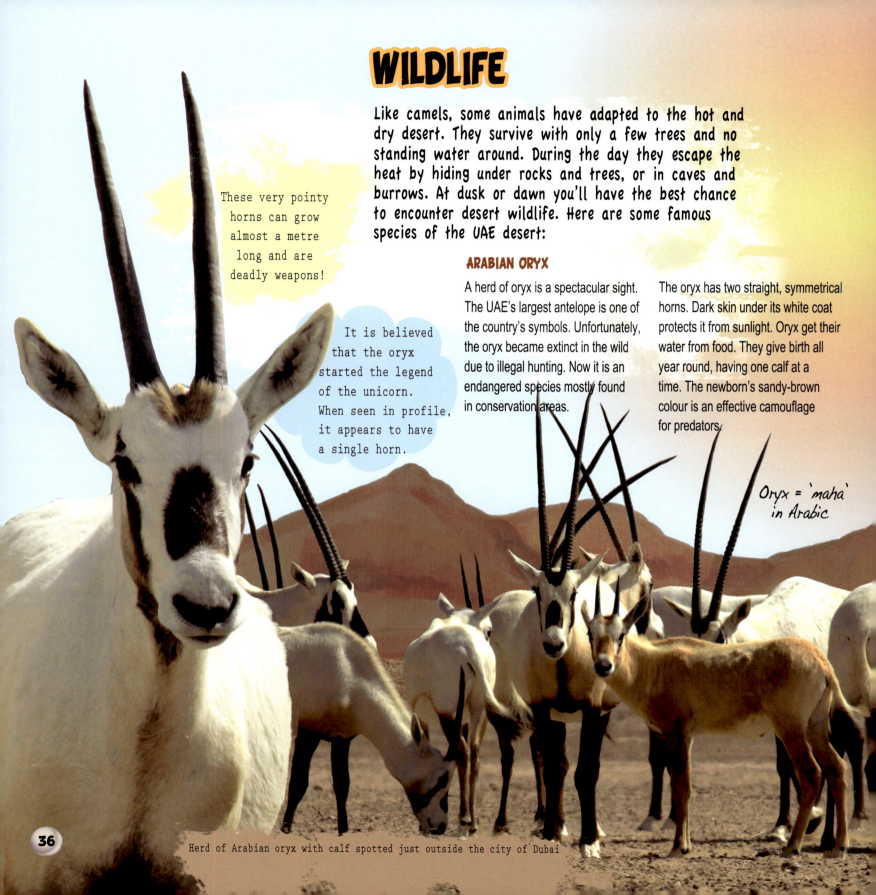

WILDLIFE

Like camels, some animals have adapted to the hot and dry desert. They survive with only a few trees and no standing water around. During the day they escape the heat by hiding under rocks and trees, or in caves and burrows. At dusk or dawn you'll have the best chance to encounter desert wildlife. Here are some famous species of the UAE desert:

These very pointy horns can grow almost a metre long and are deadly weapons!

It is believed that the oryx started the legend of the unicorn. When seen in profile, it appears to have a single horn.

ARABIAN ORYX

A herd of oryx is a spectacular sight. The UAE's largest antelope is one of the country's symbols. Unfortunately, the oryx became extinct in the wild due to illegal hunting. Now it is an endangered species mostly found in conservation areas.

The oryx has two straight, symmetrical horns. Dark skin under its white coat protects it from sunlight. Oryx get their water from food. They give birth all year round, having one calf at a time. The newborn's sandy-brown colour is an effective camouflage for predators.

Oryx = 'maha' in Arabic

Herd of Arabian oryx with calf spotted just outside the city of Dubai

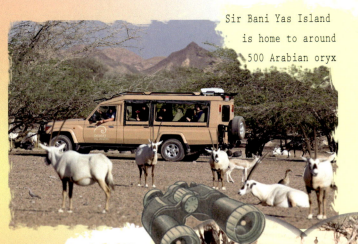

Sir Bani Yas Island is home to around 500 Arabian oryx

SPINY-TAILED LIZARD

This reptile, locally known as 'dhub', has a dinosaur-like appearance. It can grow 65cm long. Dhubs feed on shrubs and never drink water. They live in colonies and dig deep burrow systems in sand dunes. The dhub does not seek conflict. However, it can bite or strike with its spiked tail when it feels threatened.

PERFECT CAMOUFLAGE!

From a distance, sand gazelles blend in perfectly with their surroundings. It keeps them safer from predators.

Gazelles are locally also known as 'dhabi'. The capital city of the UAE, Abu Dhabi, means 'Father of Deer' in Arabic.

ARABIAN MOUNTAIN GAZELLE

is very fast, with speeds of up to 65km/h. It is recognised by the dark stripe on the flanks of its slender body. The face has beautiful markings, with two white stripes from ears to nose. Besides sandy areas, it also moves on gravel plains and in mountains, often together with four to six others.

ARABIAN SAND GAZELLE

with its curved horns, is the second largest antelope in the UAE. It is white-beige in colour. The face turns whiter as it gets older. Unlike the mountain gazelle, it does not have the dark stripe between its white belly and beige flanks. Sand gazelles are renowned for giving birth to twins.

Meet these animals in the **Al Ain Zoo**, 140km south of Dubai. Info: www.alainzoo.com.
For a close encounter with free-roaming oryx and gazelles, go on safari in the wildlife reserve of **Sir Bani Yas Island**, 250km from Abu Dhabi city. Info: www.sirbaniyasisland.com

LIFE AROUND THE CREEK

What was life like in Dubai a century ago?
Imagine the creek being the very heart of the town and a thriving port next to the Arabian Gulf. Around 20,000 inhabitants are engaged in the pearl industry, fishing or commercial trade. Wealthy merchants live in new, coral-stone windtower houses near the old fort, while most people still live in huts made of palm fronds. Dhows sail in and out of the creek, cargo is loaded and unloaded at the docks, and people meet up in bustling souks to do business or shopping.

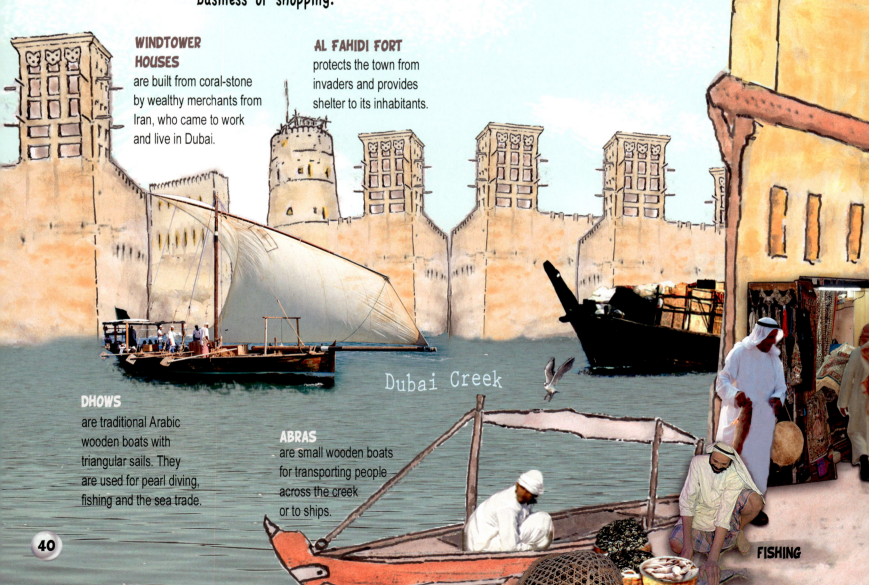

WINDTOWER HOUSES
are built from coral-stone by wealthy merchants from Iran, who came to work and live in Dubai.

AL FAHIDI FORT
protects the town from invaders and provides shelter to its inhabitants.

Dubai Creek

DHOWS
are traditional Arabic wooden boats with triangular sails. They are used for pearl diving, fishing and the sea trade.

ABRAS
are small wooden boats for transporting people across the creek or to ships.

FISHING

SOUKS

are vibrant, central marketplaces with stalls and shops where sellers, merchants and craftsmen meet their customers.

PEARL DIVING

is the main industry, providing income for the people. In the summer season, hundreds of pearling boats and their crews are found offshore, searching for oyster beds in the Arabian Gulf.

SEA TRADE

Pearls and dried fish are exported overseas to India and Iran. Products such as dates, rice, sugar, pepper, cane and wood are shipped into Dubai from as far as Eastern Africa.

PEARL DIVERS

leave the boat and decend to oyster beds up to 40m deep. They collect as many pearl oysters as they can, whilst holding their breath.

Arabian Gulf

PEARLS HERE

PALM-LEAF HOMES

Most people live in small huts made of palm leaves, called Al Arish houses or barastis.

DUBAI CREEK

Dubai's natural waterway, also known as Khor Dubai, is the heart of Dubai and the centre from which the city developed. The creek was key for early activities in fishing and pearling. It also enabled trade with other countries in the Middle East as well as to faraway places in India and East Africa. As commercial activities grew, so did the population on both banks of the creek: Bur Dubai and Deira.

Abras, the traditional boats that used to ferry people across the creek, are still operating today.

The 15km long Dubai Creek carries salty seawater from the Arabian Gulf into the heart of the city.

Dubai Creek (map label)

Arabian Gulf

Al Shindagha Tunnel

Heritage & Diving Villages

DEIRA

Gold Souk

Spice Souk

Abra station

Textile Souk

Sheikh Mohammed Centre for Cultural Understanding

BUR DUBAI

Old Souk

Abra station

Al Fahidi Fort & Dubai Museum

Dubai Creek

DREDGING THE CREEK

More than 50 years ago, the late Ruler of Dubai, Sheikh Rashid bin Saeed Al Maktoum, decided to deepen the creek. Since then, larger vessels could safely come in and Dubai became a major port in the region.

Take a boat ride and discover old and new Dubai along the creek. Hire an abra or step aboard one of the many cruise boats on the banks of the creek.

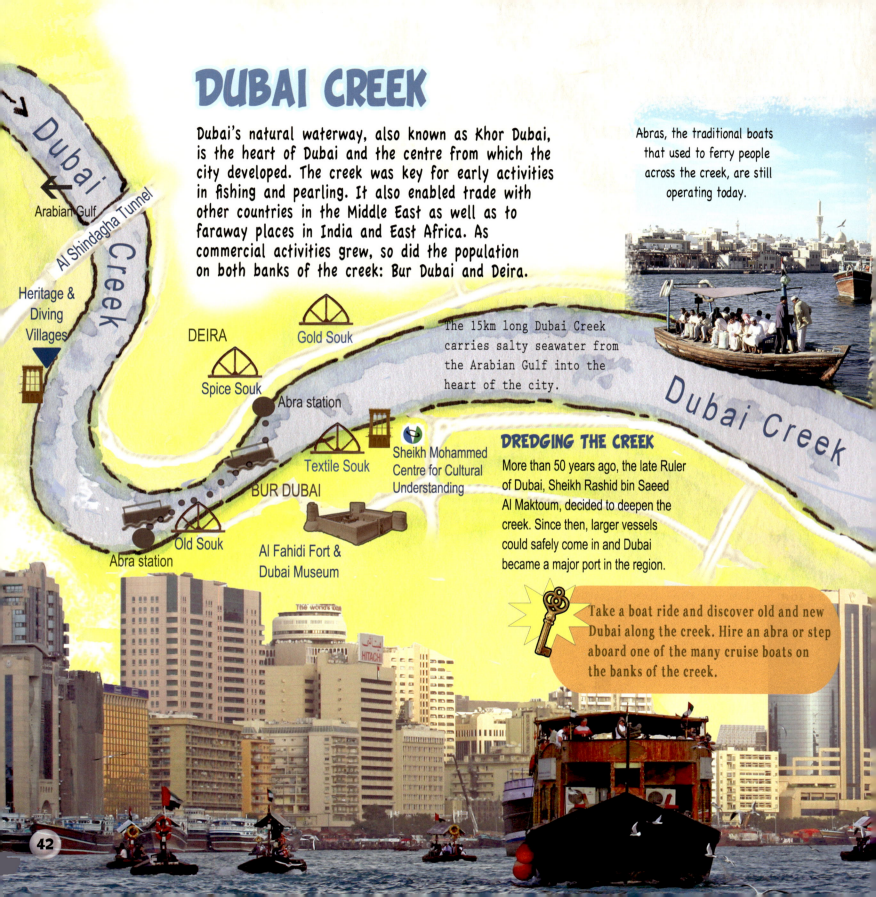

AL FAHIDI FORT

Near the creek, you will find the oldest building in Dubai, the Al Fahidi Fort. It was built around 1787 on the Bur Dubai side. The fort defended the city against invaders, such as neighbouring tribes. Throughout time, the fort has served as a seat for the government, the ruler's residence, and as a jail. Today, it is home to the Dubai Museum.

The fort's oldest tower is about 12.5m high.

DUBAI'S OLDEST BUILDING

Al Fahidi Fort was once the tallest building in Dubai. It was also the only building back then made of sea rocks and gypsum. At that time, most people lived in huts constructed from palm fronds. Later on, coral-stone houses with windtowers would appear in the neighbourhood. This historic area is part of the Al Fahidi district.

The square fort is 41m long and 33m wide with towers on three of its corners.

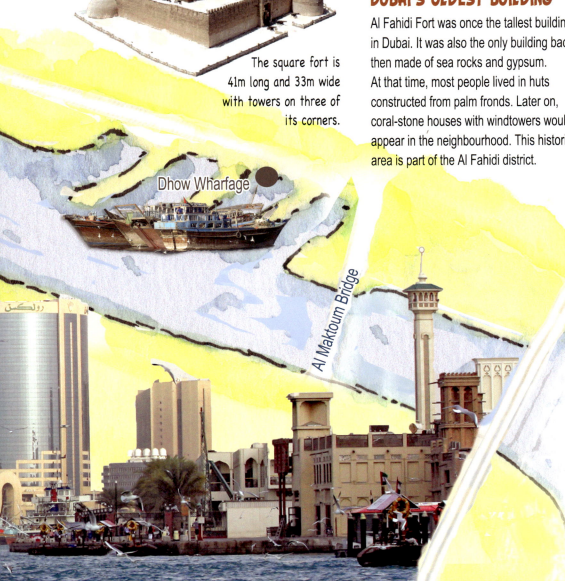

Dhow Wharfage

Al Maktoum Bridge

Today, the Al Fahidi Fort houses the Dubai Museum.

DUBAI MUSEUM

This beautiful museum is a must-see to find out more about Dubai's history. Colourful life-size dioramas with mannequins show life before the discovery of oil, such as the daily life of Bedouins, craftsmen at work in a bustling souk, and the tradition of pearl diving. Once you enter the museum you will find yourself in a large courtyard with several traditional boats on display. It also exhibits a traditional house made entirely from woven palm fronds, with a primitive windtower on top.

FISHING AND DHOWS

In past times, people living in Dubai's coastal areas made a living from the salty sea water of the Arabian Gulf and the creek. After pearl diving, fishing was the main source of income. Fishermen and pearl divers used wooden boats (dhows) with a sail to reach fishing or pearling grounds. Later, dhows would also carry traders and their goods to other countries overseas. Today, some dhows — now powered by diesel engines — still anchor in the creek. Occasionally, the wind billows the dhows' white and triangular sails during dhow racing events.

This is the story of my grandfather. He tells us his stories, Let's begin... My grandfather started to go fishing with his father in Khor Dubai (Dubai Creek) when he was 11 years old. When his father got old, he began going by himself. Years later, he got married to my beautiful grandmother Amna and they started their business. He went fishing and she sold the fish that got caught in the nets. Years went by when he had to fish for more fish, because they had eight kids. Instead of getting 10, he caught 15. Then, one day he took his children with him. They went on his small, old boat and my uncle fell in the water. My grandfather told me that my uncle's face looked so funny!

— Hareth Abdulla

Fish = 'samak' in Arabic

The vibrant Deira Fish Market in Shindagha is worth visiting. Info: www.dm.gov.ae

THE ART OF FISHING

Fishermen knew exactly where to catch different species of fish. They used fish traps made from palm fronds, dome-shaped wire traps (gargoar) or fishing nets. The nets were left overnight and fish would get trapped as they couldn't see the nets in the dark. The gargoar would lie at the bottom of the sea for several days with bait inside.

Freshly caught fish was sold on the local market, dried for export or brought home to feed the family. Fishing skills were passed down from father to son.

Gargoar

LOCAL FISH

More than 300 species of fish can be found in the waters of Dubai. Some famous ones are:

Hammour

Sheri fish

Sea bream

Fishermen arriving home with their catch on the Dubai Creek, 1963

DIFFERENT DHOWS

The first dhows were small and made from palm tree fronds, tied together with ropes, or built from a tree trunk. Later on, more materials and tools became available for the construction of larger boats. They could travel longer distances and carry more people and cargo. Smaller boats, called abras, are still used to ferry people across the creek.

DHOWS IN THE CREEK

You can still see dhows laden with cargo being docked along the creek. As nowadays most goods arrive in big container ships via Dubai's modern ports, the creek still serves as a port for sea trade with other small ports in the region.

DHOW RACING

Traditional sailing boats up to 60 feet long speed through the waves in dhow racing events. The yearly race in the UAE is called 'Al Qaffal', which means the 'journey back home'; the dhows retracing the route pearl divers would have sailed in the past.

SAMBUK
Dhow used for pearling or fishing

ABRA
A traditional wooden boat

BOOM
Deep-sea dhow used for trading

45

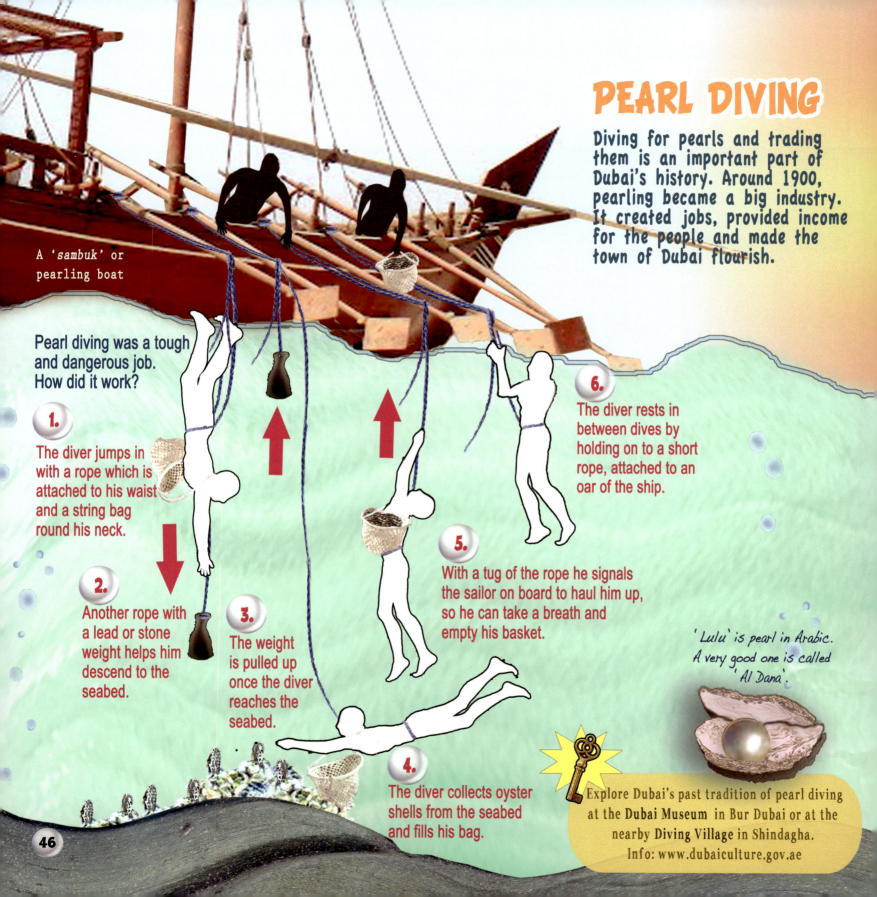

PEARL DIVING

Diving for pearls and trading them is an important part of Dubai's history. Around 1900, pearling became a big industry. It created jobs, provided income for the people and made the town of Dubai flourish.

A 'sambuk' or pearling boat

Pearl diving was a tough and dangerous job. How did it work?

1. The diver jumps in with a rope which is attached to his waist and a string bag round his neck.

2. Another rope with a lead or stone weight helps him descend to the seabed.

3. The weight is pulled up once the diver reaches the seabed.

4. The diver collects oyster shells from the seabed and fills his bag.

5. With a tug of the rope he signals the sailor on board to haul him up, so he can take a breath and empty his basket.

6. The diver rests in between dives by holding on to a short rope, attached to an oar of the ship.

'Lulu' is pearl in Arabic. A very good one is called 'Al Dana'.

Explore Dubai's past tradition of pearl diving at the **Dubai Museum** in Bur Dubai or at the nearby **Diving Village** in Shindagha. Info: www.dubaiculture.gov.ae

46

THE LIFE OF A PEARL DIVER

It's early morning in June. Ahmed is aboard one of the many boats leaving the coast onto the waters of the Arabian Gulf. He is part of an 18-man crew. The captain (nakhuda), the other divers, their pullers and sailors are all there. While moving the heavy oars in pairs of two, the men start singing. The boat will take him offshore where pearl beds can be found up to 30m deep. He should be able to reach them and hold his breath for about three minutes for each dive. After a light meal of dates, rice and fish they finally reach the diving site.

Before sunset, Ahmed is ready to make between 30 and 50 dives collecting as many oysters as he can. His puller is his companion whom he trusts to haul him up whenever he needs to come to the surface for a breath. He thinks of his dear wife and children, left behind at the coast. Ahmed comforts himself with the vision of his family cheering on the shore upon his safe return. After four months, when the pearling season is over, they will move back to the desert and spend the winter together.

Oyster shells

The pearls are sold in India and Europe by pearl merchants.

Divers use nose clips – made of turtle shell or wood – to close their nostrils. Some also wear a protective suit and gloves.

The price of a pearl depends on its colour, shape, size and weight.

Before sunset, when the diving is done, the men on board open the shells to look for pearls inside. Every man aboard gets a share of the pearl harvest. The captain, divers and their pullers receive the most.

Pearl scales

A sieve to sort out the different pearl sizes.

The UAE's pearling industry collapsed in the 1930s when Japan found a way to farm pearls.

Old Souk in Deira, 1963

SOUKS

Souks were Dubai's first marketplaces. You could find open-air or partially covered souks for fish, fruit and vegetables, spices, gold, textiles, household items and more. Craftsmen and vendors would meet their buyers there. Souks were located on both sides of the creek: Bur Dubai and Deira.
Deira Souk became Dubai's central marketplace with over 350 shops. It was once the largest souk in the region.

Fish Market in Deira, 1965

Carpenters, tailors, barbers, spice traders, iron smiths, pearl and gold merchants, textile or food vendors and many more had their own floor space, stall or shop in a souk. They were often only known by their names. One could hear clients shouting out names in search of a specific vendor.

TODAY'S SOUKS

Through time, traditional souks have been replaced by supermarkets and shopping malls. Dubai's ultra-modern versions of souks are huge and luxurious shopping malls. However, you can still experience the old days in some renovated, old-style souks. They have been restored to remind us of Dubai's early trading days. These markets with small alleys are covered with traditional wooden roofs, and the shops still have the old-style wooden doors.

The old-style souks sell local products and items from the region.

Ride a traditional abra across the creek. You'll find abra stations on both sides of the water. Enjoy a lovely five-minute boat trip for only a few dirhams. Info: www.rta.ae

48

Spice Souk

VISIT THE SOUKS

You will find both the Old Souk and Textile Souk on the Bur Dubai side of the creek. The opposite side, Deira, is the place to visit the Spice and Gold Souks. These traditional souks are great places to buy souvenirs from Dubai and the region. Use your bargaining skills to get a good price.

souvenirs

The Old Souk
in Bur Dubai

Souk Madinat Jumeirah

SOUK MADINAT JUMEIRAH

was built recently to resemble a traditional souk. It has a bazaar-like atmosphere and many alleys to wander around. You can get good quality souvenirs, but it is more expensive than in the older souks.

49

WINDTOWERS

Today, we use electrical air-conditioning systems or fans in houses to cope with hot weather. A century ago, when there was no electricity available, some houses in Dubai had windtowers on top that had similar cooling functions.

Houses in Dubai used to have small windows to prevent sunlight and sand coming inside. Sometimes a windtower, or 'barjeel', was placed three to five metres above the roof allowing breezes of fresh air with less sand to come into the room below.

The wooden cross bars of the tower were sometimes draped with wet cloths to cool the air blowing into the tower. The number of windtowers on the house indicated the wealth of the owner.

Windtower or 'barjeel'

Al Arish house (Dubai Museum)

Even some primitive houses had windtowers on top, like this summer house built out of palm tree leaves with a windtower made of burlap.

Old quarter of Bastakiya (Al Fahidi District) near the creek in Bur Dubai.

Bastakiya (Al Fahidi District) now houses museums, galleries, cafés and small hotels.

BASTAKIYA (AL FAHIDI DISTRICT)

At the end of the 19th century, people from Bastak (Iran) came to Dubai to work as textile traders or pearl merchants. They built windtower houses along the creek. This neighbourhood is part of the Al Fahidi historic district, also known as Bastakiya. The windtower houses are packed closely together. The high walls and small lanes (sikkas) give maximum shade on the ground.

Explore the labyrinth of alleyways in Al Fahidi, or join a tour from the Sheikh Mohammed Centre for Cultural Understanding. Info: www.cultures.ae

HOW DOES IT WORK?

1) This windtower has four vents. They will capture the wind coming from any direction.

2) It catches the wind high above the ground where the air is cooler and less laden with sand.

3) The air speeds up through this funnel and enters the room below.

4) The fresh air circulates in the room so people can enjoy a nice, cool breeze.

5) The used air leaves the building through the three remaining vents.

How smart: air-conditioning without electricity !

Unique in the UAE: the round windtower of Sharjah.

Majlis al Midfaa

Villa on The Palm Jumeirah

Madinat Jumeirah

Windtowers are still used to decorate modern buildings such as houses and hotels. They have lost their function since powerful air-conditioning systems have taken over.

DESERT THRILLS

The Dubai desert has beautiful, reddish-orange sand dunes, as you will see on the road to Hatta. The wind gives the dunes their spectacular wave-like shapes that grow higher nearer the mountains. There are many ways to enjoy the sand dunes...

UNIQUE COLOUR

The unique rusty-red colour comes from oxidated iron in the sand.

QUAD BIKING

CAMPING

ENJOYING THE SAND DUNES

There are many ways to have fun in the desert. Bashing the dunes in a 4x4 car, camping overnight, roasting marshmallows over the campfire, gazing at the dark sky filled with stars...

The desert is stunning and safe if you bring a 4x4 car and plenty of drinking water with you. A towing cable and accompanying cars will help in case you get stuck in the deep sand.

STAR GAZING

DESERT DRIVING

CAMEL RIDING

SAND BOARDING

DUNE BASHING

Help to keep our desert clean! Leave nothing but your footprints behind.

Many companies in Dubai organise all-inclusive **desert safaris.** You can even enjoy an overnight stay in a desert camp.

55

FUN AND INTERESTING PLACES

Water parks, beaches, ski slopes, museums, souks... Indoors or outdoors, there are plenty of things to do in and around Dubai – places for having fun as well as museums and heritage sites to explore the UAE's rich culture and history. This map shows you the locations of some fun and interesting places worth visiting while you are here.

Some places have a key and page number referring to tips and information on previous pages of the book.

Aquaventure Water park

Arabian

Wild Wadi Water park

The Lost Chambers

The Beach

Atlantis

PALM JUMEIRAH

Souk Madinat

Abu Dhabi ←

JBR Dubai Marina

Sheikh Zayed Road

Umm Suqeim

E11

Sheikh Zayed Grand Mosque

About 120km south-west of Dubai

ABU DHABI

Emirates Golf Club

Mall of the Emirates & Ski Dubai

EVENTS IN DUBAI

The Rugby Sevens, Dubai World Cup, the Emirates Airline Festival of Literature, camel races and the Dubai Shopping Festival are just some of the many events that Dubai hosts every year. Check what's coming up next on **www.dubaicalendar.ae**

31

Abu Dhabi Falcon Hospital

Yas Waterworld Abu Dhabi

E311

Dubai Miracle Garden

37

Sir Bani Yas Island

Ferrari World Abu Dhabi

AL AIN

37

About 140km south of Dubai ↓

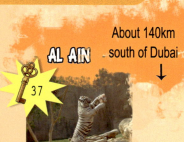

Al Ain Zoo

Sheikh Mohammed Bin Z

Global Village

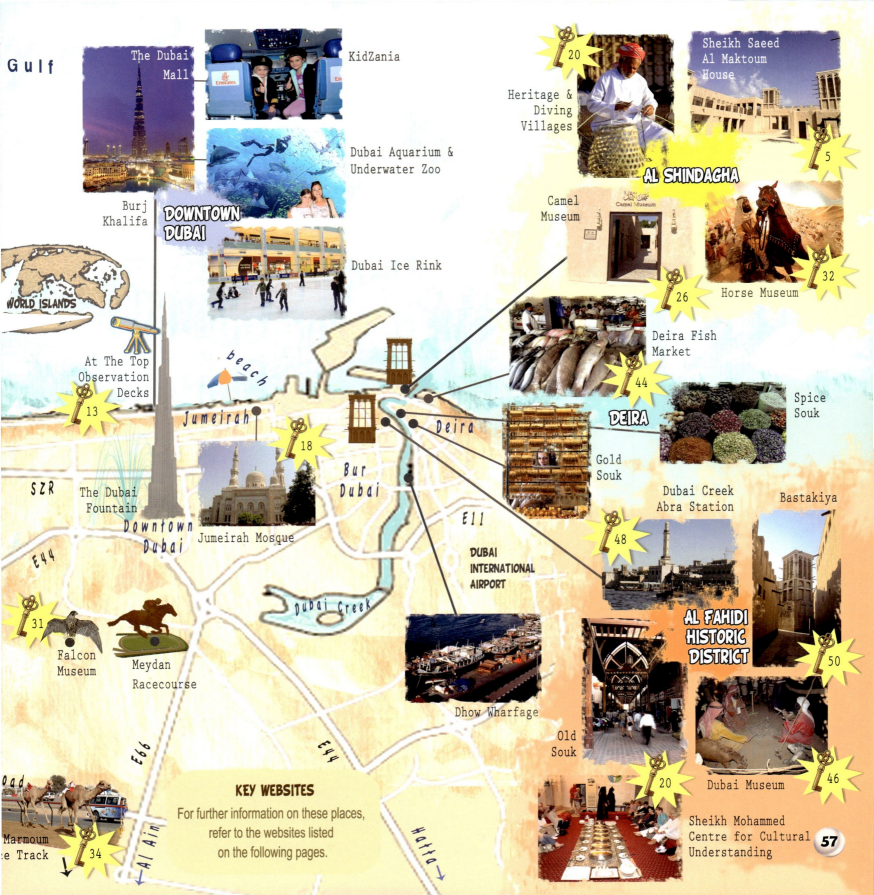

Gulf

The Dubai Mall

KidZania

Dubai Aquarium & Underwater Zoo

Burj Khalifa

DOWNTOWN DUBAI

Dubai Ice Rink

WORLD ISLANDS

At The Top Observation Decks

13

beach

Jumeirah

18

SZR

The Dubai Fountain

Downtown Dubai

Jumeirah Mosque

E44

31

Falcon Museum

Meydan Racecourse

Bur Dubai

E11

Dubai Creek

Dubai International Airport

Dhow Wharfage

Old Souk

20

Heritage & Diving Villages

20

Sheikh Saeed Al Maktoum House

5

AL SHINDAGHA

Camel Museum

Horse Museum

32

26

Deira Fish Market

44

DEIRA

Spice Souk

Gold Souk

Dubai Creek Abra Station

Bastakiya

48

AL FAHIDI HISTORIC DISTRICT

50

Dubai Museum

46

Marmoum e Track

34

Al Ain

Hatta

KEY WEBSITES
For further information on these places,
refer to the websites listed
on the following pages.

Sheikh Mohammed Centre for Cultural Understanding

WEBSITES

Abu Dhabi Falcon Hospital
www.falconhospital.com

Al Ain Zoo
www.alainzoo.ae

Aquaventure water park
www.atlantisthepalm.com

Bastakiya
www.cultures.ae

Burj Khalifa At The Top observation deck
www.burjkhalifa.ae

Calendar of events in Dubai
www.dubaicalendar.ae

Dubai Aquarium & Underwater Zoo
www.thedubaiaquarium.com

Dubai Government
www.dubai.ae

Dubai Ice RInk
www.dubaiicerink.com

Dubai Miracle Garden
www.dubaimiraclegarden.com

Falcon Museum in Dubai
www.dm.gov.ae

Ferrari World Abu Dhabi
www.ferrariworldabudhabi.com

Fish Market Deira
www.dm.gov.ae

Global Village
www.globalvillage.ae

Jumeirah Mosque
www.cultures.ae

KidZania
www.kidzania.ae

Meydan
www.meydan.ae

Museums and heritage sites in Dubai
www.dubaiculture.gov.ae

News and information on the UAE
www.uaeinteract.com

Public transport in Dubai
www.rta.ae

Sheikh Mohammed Centre for Cultural Understanding (SMCCU)
www.cultures.ae

Sheikh Zayed Grand Mosque Abu Dhabi
www.szgmc.ae

Sir Bani Yas Island
www.sirbaniyasisland.com

Ski Dubai
www.skidubai.com

Souk Madinat Jumeirah
www.madinatjumeirah.com

The Beach
www.thebeach.ae

The Dubai Fountain
www.thedubaimall.com

The Dubai Mall
www.thedubaimall.com

The Lost Chambers
www.atlantisthepalm.com

Tourist information and attractions
www.visitdubai.com

Wild Wadi water park
www.wildwadi.com

Yas Waterworld Abu Dhabi
www.yaswaterworld.com

Sheikh Mohammed Centre for Cultural Understanding (SMCCU)

A great way to truly experience the Emirati culture, customs and religion, is through the activities offered by the Sheikh Mohammed Centre for Cultural Understanding (SMCCU).

Join a traditional Emirati meal in the centre's old windtower house, visit the beautiful Jumeirah Mosque or let your guide take you through the alleyways of the historic neighbourhood. The centre is located in Bastakiya, part of the Al Fahidi historic district in Bur Dubai. For a calendar of events and bookings, see: www.cultures.ae

Open doors. Open minds.

Sheikh Mohammed bin Rashid Centre
for Cultural Understanding

الأبواب مفتوحة. العقول متفتحة.
مركز الشيخ محمد بن راشد آل مكتوم
للتواصل الحضاري

ACKNOWLEDGEMENTS

Creating this book has been a wonderful venture thanks to the support and contribution of many others.
I am grateful for the shared enthusiasm and participation of family and friends, and people I have met along
the way. In particular I would like to thank Hareth and Amani Abdulla, Gillian Byron, Tracey Flook, Wouter
Kingma, Hetty Post, Nienke Salomons, and Patricia and Annabelle Verhagen.

A variety of experts and organisations in different fields and photographers also contributed to this book.
I would like to gratefully acknowledge the following for their share of knowledge, their expert advice
and accuracy checks on the text:
Nasif Kayed, Dr Margit Muller, Amal Murad, Len Chapman, Ludwig Hejze, Salman Bushelaibi, May Hamid,
Taha Al Hamri, Sarah Smit, Kate Shanahan, Marti Hardin, Al Sahra Desert Resort Equestrian Centre,
the conservation team of Sir Bani Yas (TDIC), The Emirates Group, Jumeirah Group, Emaar Properties,
Ski Dubai and Van Oord.

I would like to thank the following for their artistic contributions and permission to reproduce photographs:

Illustrations: Annabelle Verhagen, 15(mr), 20(tl).
Photographs: Cover: Sashkinw/Dreamstime.com - Golden Key in Keyhole Photo;
Photographs provided courtesy of the Government of Dubai, Department of Tourism and Commerce Marketing:
4(tr), 4(bl), 4(mm), 4(br), 6(mm), 8 and 9(t), 11(tl), 11(mm), 11(mr), 11(bl), 12(br), 13(tr), 21(tr), 21(bm), 30(bl), 42(tr),
44(tl), 44(bm), 45(tr), 45(mr), 45(bl), 45(br), 49(tl), 49(bl), 51(bl), 56(mr), 57(tl), 57(tr), 57(mm), 57(bm), 57(br);
Abu Dhabi Falcon Hospital, 31; Alison Webster, 21(mr), 35(tr); Amal Murad (REDAA), 17(bl); Anantara, 37(tl), 56(bl);
Anita van der Krol/www.anitavanderkrol.com, 5(tl); Anne Maartje Metz, 17(tr), 50(bl); 57(mr); Annemarie Leenart, 6(mr);
Arabian Water Parks, 56(mm); Atlantis, The Palm, 56(tm); Celia Peterson/arabianeye.com, p14(bm); Cor Verheij, 9(mr),
10(mr), 12(tl), 18(mm), 5(mr), 42/43(b); Dubai Media Office, 33(tm), 33(ml); Dubai Miracle Garden, 56(mr); Ferrari World
Abu Dhabi, 56(bl); Global Village, 56(br); Heidi de Haas, 10(tl); Hetty Post/www.toursforyoudubai.com, 51(mr);
Jessy Loockx/Arabian Stud Europe, 33(br); Jumeirah Group/Online Media Library, 11(tm), 40(ml), 45(ml), 47(tl), 56(tr);
Len Chapman/www.dubaiasitusedtobe.com, 4(mr), 5(tr), 48(tl); Ludwig Hejze, 45(tl), 48(ml); Mare van der
Hoeven, 9(mm); Marieke Vreeburg, 57(tm); National Archives, 30(tr); Nienke Keizer, 9(ml); Nienke Salomons/Dubai
Culture & Arts Authority, 25(bl), 28(bm); Sarah Smit, vi/vii, 32(bl), 37(tr), 37(mr); Sheikh Mohammed Centre for Cultural
Understanding, 59; Sjoerd Leenart, 13(bm); Ski Dubai, 11(tr); Susanne Baltes, 54(mr); Sylvia van Roey/arabianeye.com,
47(bl);Tanja Nijhuis, 36(b); The Emirates Group, v, 5(tr), 6(br), 7(bm); Timo Elliott/www.timoelliott.com, 55(mr); Van Oord,
11(ml), 11(bm); Yas Waterworld Abu Dhabi, 56(bl).

ABOUT THE AUTHOR

Liliane van der Hoeven was born and raised in The Netherlands. Over 15 years, Liliane and her family lived in Taiwan and Hungary and since 2010, she has been living in Dubai. During her years as an expat, Liliane came to realise the importance, especially for children, of understanding the culture of the country they live in which might be very different to their home country. While relocating to new places in the world, she learnt that books are great tools for helping her own three children settle and understand their new surroundings.

Liliane completed a Masters in Educational Science in The Netherlands. Following her studies, she developed a career in PR and communication, consulting and graphic design. She ran her own PR and communication agency in The Netherlands before she moved abroad. While being an expat she has taken on several advisory and committee roles in international schools.

Today, creating children's books is her passion and one with which she can combine her background in education with her design/communication skills. Liliane's first book, *Footprints in Dubai*, was published in 2012 and allows international children to create a keepsake of their Dubai life and friendships. The success of her first book encouraged Liliane to write *The Key to Dubai*. She has put her time, artistic talent and writing skills into producing Dubai's first-ever children's encyclopedia, bursting with facts and images about Dubai and the Emirati culture.

GLOSSARY

A

Abaya – black, long and loose dress worn by Emirati women

Abra – traditional boat made of wood, used to ferry people across the creek

Abu Dhabi – capital city of the United Arab Emirates

Adhaan – call to prayer usually through a loudspeaker from the mosque

Agal – black cord to keep a man's headscarf in place

Al Dana – a very good pearl

Al Khamsa – bloodlines of the Arabian horse

Al Qaffal – annual, traditional dhow race event in the UAE

Allah – Arabic word for God

Arish house – house made of palm fronds for summer living

Ayyala dance – traditional dance of war performed by men

B

Barasti – house constructed from palm leaves

Barjeel – Arabic word for windtower

Bastakiya – old quarter in the historic Al Fahidi district of Dubai

Bedouins – nomadic people living in the desert

Bin/bint – Arabic for son/daughter of

Bisht – traditional loose robe for men, worn over the kandoura

Boom – large cargo dhow for seatrade

Burlap – strong, rough cloth usually made of jute

Burqa – mask for women that covers most of the face

C

Camel – Arabian camel with one hump, also called dromedary

Camel racing – traditional sport of running camels at speed over a track

Camouflage – blending in with the surroundings to remain unnoticed

Cardamom – aromatic spice used to flavour Arabic coffee and food

Charity – the act of doing good or helping others

Creek – inlet of the sea

Custom – rule that is socially enforced

D

Dallah – classic Arabic coffee pot with beak

Dana – a very good pearl

Dates – fruit from the date palm

Dhow – traditional Arabian sailing boat, made of wood

Dhub – desert lizard

Dirham – currency of the United Arab Emirates

Dome – hollow upper half of a sphere, architectural shape

Dromedary – one-humped camel

Dubai – emirate and biggest city in the UAE

Dune bashing – off-road driving on sand dunes

E

Emirate – the state or territory that is ruled by an Emir or Sheikh

Emiratis – local people of the United Arab Emirates

Emirati dress – national dress worn by local people in the UAE

Endurance – the ability or strength to keep on going

Expatriate (expat) – a person living in a country other than his/her home country

F

Falaj – system of canals and wells that supplies water for drinking and irrigation

Falconry – tradition of hunting by means of a trained falcon

Fasting – refraining from drinking or eating

G

Gahwah – Arabic coffee

Gaimat – crunchy dough balls with date molasses

Gargoar – dome-shaped wire trap used for fishing

Ghafiyah – tight (embroidered) men's hat or cap worn underneath a headscarf

Ghutra – headscarf for men

H

Hajj – pilgrimage made by Muslims to Mecca

Halal – anything that is permitted under Islamic law

Henna – a shrub that is used to dye hair or decorate hands and feet

Hindi – language widely spoken in India

Hisaan – Arabic word for horse

Hospitality – making guests or strangers feel welcome

Houbara – bustard, prey of the falcon

I

Iftar feast – festive dinner after sunset during fasting (Ramadan)
Imam – the man who leads the prayers in a mosque
Indigo – blue colour dye extracted from plants
Islam – religion of Muslims

J

Jamal – Arabic word for camel
Jockey – someone that rides horses or camels

K

Kandoura – long and loose robe, worn by Emirati men

L

Legend – a traditional story or belief
Lulu – Arabic word for pearl

M

Maha – Arabic word for oryx
Majlis – place or room where people gather
Marhaba – Arabic word for welcome and hello
Masjid – Arabic for mosque
Mecca – birthplace of Prophet Mohammad, city in Saudi Arabia
Mihrab – niche or arch in the wall of a mosque showing the direction to Mecca
Minaret – tower on a mosque
Mosque – house of prayer for Muslims
Muezzin – person who calls Muslims to prayer
Muslim – person who follows the religion of Islam

N

Na'ashat dance – dance for young women swaying their hair
Nakhuda – captain of a (pearling) boat
Nomads – people that move from one place to another

O

Oasis – fertile area in a desert where water is found

P

Pearl diving – collecting oysters from the seabed in seach for pearls
Pillars of Islam – five rules or core beliefs for Muslim life
Predator – an animal that hunts and feeds on prey

Prophet Mohammad – messenger of God, according to Muslim belief

Q

Quibla – wall in a mosque that faces Mecca
Quran – Holy book of Islam

R

Ramadan – Holy month of fasting

S

Saffron – expensive spice with yellow thread used for taste and colour
Saluki – fast and slender hunting dog
Samak – Arabic word for fish
Sambuk – pearling boat
Sheikh – tribal leader or ruler, means 'elder' (sheikha for women)
Sheila/shayla – headscarf for women
Shindagha – historical area at the mouth of Dubai Creek
Sikka – narrow alleyway
Skyscraper – very tall building of many floors
Souk – marketplace or bazaar

T

Tagalog – language spoken in the Philippines
Tarboush – decorative tassel hanging from the kandoura's collar
Tawa – roasting pan for coffee beans
Thawb – see kandoura
Tradition – something you do because your (grand)parents also did it
Turmeric – old Indian spice with a warm, bitter taste used to colour and flavour food

U

Unicorn – horse-like animal from a traditional story with one straight horn on its forehead
United Arab Emirates – federation of seven emirates in the Middle East
Urdu – language mainly spoken in Pakistan and India

W

Wadi – dry riverbed or valley that fills up after rain
Windtower – cooling tower on top of a house

INDEX

BIBLIOGRAPHY

Camel Race Keeps Cultural Roots Alive Cheryl Robertson, GulfNews, 2013 available from: http://gulfnews.com/gn-focus/-uae-national-day/camel-race-keeps-cultural-roots-alive-1.1262009

Camel Racing in the United Arab Emirates Sulayman Khalaf, Ethnology, University of Pittsburgh, 2000 available from: http://sites.uci.edu/arabsocietyandcultures/files/2011/09/Khalaf-Camel-Racing-in-UAE.pdf

Don't they know it's Friday? Jeremy Williams, Motivate Publishing, 1998

Elements of Culture Sheikh Mohammed Centre for Cultural Understanding available from: http://www.cultures.ae

History of Dubai available from: http://www.sheikhmohammed.com

Pioneers in The Pearl Trade, The Arabs available from: http://blogs.houseofgems.com/index.php/2012/10/pioneers-in-the-pearl-trade-the-arabs/

Population Bulletin Emirate of Dubai 2013 Dubai Statistics Center, February 2014

Population Estimates 2006-2010 Report, United Arab Emirates National Bureau of Statistics

Roots of the Union Abu Dhabi Authority for Culture & Heritage

Sheikh Zayed Frances LaBonte, Jerboa Books, 2006

Telling Tales: An Oral History of Dubai Julia Wheeler & Paul Thuysbaert, Explorer Publishing & Distribution, 2010

The Illustrated Encyclopedia of Arabia Mary Beardwood, Stacey International, 2008

The Pearl Diver Julia Johnson, Stacey International, 2009

Traditions available from www.uaeinteract.com

What do you know about the United Arab Emirates & the Emirati National?
Salem Humaid, Almezmaah Studies and Research Center, 2012

Windtowers Gulf Architecture available from www.catnaps.org/islamic/gulfarch4